Muzzle

Muzzle

Rivka Clifton

JACKLEG PRESS

JackLeg Press
www.jacklegpress.org

Copyright © 2025 by Rivka Clifton.
Published 2025 by JackLeg Press. All rights reserved.
Printed in the United States of America.

ISBN: 978-1-956907148

Library of Congress Control Number: 2023945618

Cover Credits:
Image by Brett Lindell
Model—Soft Abilez
Clothing—UNK by Corvette

Praise For Muzzle

Welcome to Muzzle: Rivka Clifton's kaleidoscopic meditation on the viscerality of language. In this collection, Clifton braids a knack for choice diction and phrasing with a distinct facility for image-driven narrative and delivers poems that evoke emotional nuance and depth. The urgency behind these poems is like that of the pulse: insistent, carnal, necessary. These poems explore the multiple meanings of its title word, the various definitions and uses acting out how each word is "[a] body within a body," shifting and restless. These poems take on as truth that the "tongue is a mysterious beast— / all it loves plummets down the throat"—and follow this sensorial understanding of language down into surreal yet eerily familiar depths.

—José Angel Araguz, author of *Rotura*

Rivka Clifton's debut poetry collection, Muzzle, teaches us to wrap fear around our shoulders like a haunted shawl. To our delight, this keeps us warm, as even the most innocuous things—leaves on a lawn, a stray hair, even the moon and stars in various iterations—become sinister and foreboding. Clifton's poetry thins the threshold between human and beast, nightmare and joyful epiphany.

—Mary Biddinger, author of *Department of Elegy*

In Rivka Clifton's riveting debut Muzzle, one can feel the bristling gravity of concision and the turning of a blade in each carved line. This visceral collection navigates desire, trauma, the slipperiness of the self, and the out-of-body horror of the mundane. The speakers of these poems twist and morph, at once husband, wife, child, hunter, animal, myth, and the dark itself calling through a kind of god-mouth, consuming all. In these stunning dreamscapes, flowers bloom into a brain, lightning unchains a boy's teeth, and the "delicate Morse/inside a throat" hammers against the page. Simultaneously enchanting and frightening, Muzzle invites us to re-see our apocalyptic worlds and reckon with the animal impulses rippling under our own skin.

—Hadara Bar-Nadav, author of *The Animal is Chemical*

Contents

(n) *The opening at the end of the barrel of a firearm; the end part of a gun barrel nearest to its opening.*

(n) *The projecting part of the head of an animal, including the nose and jaws.*

(n) *a device, usually an arrangement of straps or wires, placed over an animal's mouth to prevent the animal from biting, eating, etc.*

(v) *To restrain from speaking; to impose silence on; to suppress the message of.*

Borgman

After a lifetime
away, I return to

the taut strings
of the Midwest.

Its white sheds
bruise with evening.

Each tooth in
a dog's mouth

pulling a long
note from a carcass.

Muzzle

Clouds stretch
unreachable webs

across the tree-line.
Maples shed
their cardinal leaves.

A pack of hunters
lies prone in the field.

A cloud spills grey
oil over their guns.

They aim at a wolf,
who, a second ago,
was someone's son.

I am someone
who has held a gun.

The Void, a Body Once

The delicate morse
inside a throat

hammers its flesh
against flesh.

Muted pads

thrum through the black

tombstones
of wet cedars.

A body runs
from a hunter

mouth and eyes wide

its heart's wet suck
      like a rag

wrung tight and dripping.

Its pulse sings
        through its throat.

It cannot stop

its radio-wave
call to tear away
the ground.

The earth's chest
groans
        a paw

pushes through soil

and the void
a body once filled

becomes
a crosshatch
        of limbs.

Devil in The Backyard

He parts his hair
    down the middle
        to show us his eye-

sized zit. He squeezes

        the last drops of juice
from a lime wedge

into his gin and gin.
Would you like a sip?

We would
    rather not
        refuse.

    He spits
  into his palm
and says lick.

We feel his horns
inside our mouths.
    We stretch

our lips
back and see
molars.

He sets his bones

in a posthole outside.
He says squat.

He traces his zit
with a cigarette butt.
Hordes of flies

on his vinyl siding
shake their wings.
We run through

his yard, barefoot,
sparklers
in hand.

Back inside,
corpse pose.

He presses our lips
to his mug.

Since we are good
for nothing,

      we swallow.

Faithful is The Wounding

When I tilt the cup
it drains like a face.

Outside
in the yard
my children

strut like grackles.
My wife

decapitates a toad
with the lawn mower.

She stoops
and tosses the body
into the street.

She continues
to erase the lawn

blade by blade.
Juice spills over
my hand.

Washing dishes,
I erase what

we as a family
have left.

Within Him

Unsure
about the dark
my eyes rolled

around the room.
My son crawled out

from under
the bed.
He tucked

the blankets
around me.
When he stopped

moving he
disappeared.
My son who

unchains
lightning
from his teeth.

*

As a parent
I sat on the edge.

My son was somewhere

else
unafraid.

Each
second sliced
the dark.

Within
another's

mind for once my son

a tornado
in the back yard.

*

I served my son
a sandwich.

I dropped
it where
he sat

in the kitchen
the garbage

overflowed.
My son

in the other
room my hand

crammed down
the trash's throat.

Boxcutter

You stand at the opposite end of the aisle. Because there's an overwhelming pain in your stomach, you stumble forward. You yell. You turn to yourself. You are not yourself. You pull a knife through the air. You feel yourself mirror yourself. There is no knife. In one deft movement, you sink your knife into your stomach and glide it from one side to the other: its stinging grinds through your torso. You fall to your knees. You look up. No you. Coffee spills over the floor.

Own

In the kitchen, you hold a pepper like a heart before dropping it in the skillet. There, it pumps at regular intervals. It sizzles. *I have to find who owns this heart*, you say. Sure, you bought the heart. Light pulses across its surface. Your face glows orange. You watch the heart. It's no longer yours. You inhale the smell—then it is—yours.

If You Say It's a Dream, Then It Doesn't Count

I held a flower that bloomed
into a human brain. Curious

the things we see in things—

a sheet unfurling above
the mattress before falling

like a glove to muzzle
a disobedient snout.

There were nights I sat
on the corner of my bed,
feet not touching the floor.

I watched my pillow turn
into a baby and back again.

I saw bodies hanging
from wires in the closet.

I slipped into the shallow
pond, let the carp rub me

clean with their muscled gold,

their wild chrysanthemum
heads. Outside, the night's

ungloved hand rotated
a vision like a crystal ball
on the tips of its fingers.

It took the smoke from all
the burning piles of leaves

to wrap around its neck.

Hanger

His breathless ribcage splayed, wispy flesh
                    corseted, single crease
in the forehead. For him, no joy just crush
            and bone jut. No one wanted

my gifts: diapers, nursing pads, cancelled
        appointments. Everyone asked.
What do we sing for disappointment?
            The barn doors opened,

their hammering song; bones and nails
                    buried deep
                            in wood.

Faithful is The Wounding

In his carrier, my husband
pants and spins. He howls

as we curve around country roads.
Soon, trees replace houses; we are alone.
I carry my husband into the woods.

When I reach a clearing,
I put him down. My husband

tests the dirt with his hands, his nose.
He whimpers. *Go*, I say, *I don't want you
anymore*. He looks at me, and we know

when we see each other again
he will bare his teeth.

It Doesn't Sound Good at All

Now and then, I examine
        my body. I look for marks,
for evidence that I've been marked.

Honesty is important and something

        I am capable of.
        Just the other day, I was honestly

thinking in a basement
        technically I was buried.
        The earth loomed overhead

and all around. I was on my back
        and beneath my body

a blanket. I stretched my limbs, undoing

        what the day had done
to them. When I was done

        I dragged the blanket
        up the stairs like a magician

hacking up an endless rag.

Outside—a band of trees
    the neighborhood kids

call a forest. I know something
        burrowed in the roots
is ready to surface, waiting to

    surround us, to transform
        its body into a cymbal.

Tar

On his hand,
what is a finger
but a snake

unhinging its coils?
In his mouth,

what is a tongue
but a wet foxtail
that writhes

between iron teeth?

*

New Years Eve—
he doesn't like the mercurial

shine inside
a champagne flute,

so he becomes
the cuckoo clock
on a nail in our
living room.

Every hour, he forces his wooden bird

in and out
of its zippy
mechanical door.

*

How have I fallen in love

with crossing
and uncrossing
my legs?

I can't remember

ever sucking so hard
at the air above my bed

as when I saw him,
years after his death,
pinned to the ceiling,

washed in a tar that snaked

from the corners
of his mouth
into mine.

Helicopter

You and your son are lost in the woods. It's getting dark. The trees shake. *Is it a helicopter?* Your son has glasses, but he lost them, so his eyesight can't be trusted. The trees keep shaking. Soon, it'll be too dark to see. *It must be a helicopter*, you say, but you can't be sure. Not here, with all these limbs reaching out of the dark to snag you. You look at your son, crouched down like a helicopter has come. You mirror him. You gesture as if directing a plane down a runway. If your son could see, he would be assured, he would know you were about to be pulled into the sky.

Nightride

The night runs its tongue
over itself. Black jeans,
black jacket, as dangerous
as it gets. The night swings
its dark fringe. It burns
its initials into a plastic
slide. Since the night tires
of being itself, it yawns;
its tongue leaps out
and curls around the base
of a tree.

Muzzle

The tongue is a mysterious beast—

all it loves plummets down the throat.

Once I saw a semi
jackknifed along a highway. I joked
we were about to see the dead,
and we did. In the diner,

a trucker gnaws through dry prime rib.

He knows why
the waitress cries as she replaces
the industrial-sized coffee filter.

In the season cottonwood tufts
congregate behind open doors,

I learned what gravity lures
from a mouth. His arm, popped open
with glass, hung where his sedan's door
was obliterated. This was June,

and six months before I skated
to the center of a frozen pond
and listened to the ice split

like a shoulder jerked from its socket.

Faithful is The Wounding

It's hard to trust the rugged
tree-lined cul-de-sac in October.

The leaves mimic sparrows—
the narcotic quivering
after their bodies crumple

across a windshield.
The neighbors have raked,

but I haven't. A shock
of orange in piles
shakes its desiccated face.

My husband
in the distance;

his leaf blower sputters,
the choke slowly disengaged.

The Nature of Punishment

All around the leaves
hang their concave bodies.
They wait for the wind
to fill them and heap them.
Sleep is not always
the answer eyes ask for.
Sometimes it is
a twitching orange leaf,
a flame gorged on wind
jumping from one branch
to the next.

Looking for Someone Who's Not Around

The dog pulling its chain

at the end of the block
        whipped its head back

and forth. At the fence
the dead shimmied

their trinkets. I found

        answers in a spiral
notebook. In the dark

I pulled the sheets, stretched

them over my mouth.
        I sucked in.

The dog on its chain;
the dead in unison.

        Diary, last night
my head was taken for a spin

on another's opened palm.
All night, I barked

at nothing. The dead showed me

the back of their necks.
        I spat into my hand

and swirled ink into
a mouth—always a mouth

        when I'm done with it.

By Rivers

All the stones I have ever thrown
line the bottom of the Missouri.
Scales, tiny convex mirrors,

stars. They never hit my retinas
because Omaha's amber light muzzles
the dark-throated sky. The night I turned 20

on the library floor, I couldn't move.
The soft light breathed in the corners.
Who is like the Lord?

The swallower of a hundred river snakes
is like the Lord. She wades into the Missouri.
She snags a snake. She opens—her throat

tuned to the river's thickened bending.

A Cicada Sings at Night to Avoid Predators

Those nights, the thermometer never slipped below
ninety. Those nights coughed up a white husk

of a boy. He wheezed through his gaping mouth,
a rose stuffed with another rose. He had no home.

The boy smelled like heat gathering in a feather.
His hands were empty. No. They held his voice.

He unhinged his jaw not into a grin but something giddy
and contorted, a gash that glowed vermillion.

They said his home was swallowed
in a fire, a storm, a sinkhole.

The Hour of The Wolf

Your chest pulsed. Your ribs rippled under your skin as if a pebble were thrown into your navel. You left the cul-de-sac. You entered the woods. Every neighborhood has a story like this—a husk between the tree trunks, a voice that calls from the unmoving body. You waded into a nearby stream. Your eyes alone bobbed on the surface as your body cut through the water, hissing. Yes, you hissed. They said you were not human, but you are. You were. The river swallowed your pale head and spat it out again.

The Bedroom

In the dark, you could mistake many things for a person: a coat draped over a chair, a chair toppled to the floor, the floor disappearing into the room's corners. In the shadows, who has hands wrapped in silk? The fiddle? The wolf? A silent scuttling weaves a new wallpaper around your room while you uncover a lump in the body of your bed.

Folding Coats

Let's separate form from function

button by button.

Along the rim
of each hole
frayed black cloth
    frays further.

Finger hook
        pull and fold

the bodies worn
underneath

a soft shell.

*

In a Christmas movie

a man splits open

the black cloth that shrouds the future.

He sees its human-shaped organs

barely ribcaged and a light
        spilling out.

A coat is nothing

but what it shrouds

fabric piled up
on the unused side
        of the bed.

*

A smoke plume
is a black coat

spread across the sky.

The evening turns
    up its collar

to the stars'
shriveled ears.

I separate
the lapels

and free what's inside.

Night sprawls
    across the bed.

Faithful is The Wounding

In the dark, the records were turning
                    dead wax into static—its fine blue
            light, the music below its hiss.

                    The basement curled
            into itself like a segmented worm.

Once my body was a room for rent:

one word and then another
                    burrowed in the hollow stomach.
            The children were asleep;

                    the stereo turned low.
            The basement wavered before

retracting its immeasurable body into the night's

wet sand. It had been months. It had
                    been years. How many?
            I could not count. But still,

                    this body within a body—

a fish tank and a ragworm.

In the basement, I turned as if a metal spindle

were lodged within. The dark,
              like a needle, dragged
       across me—its diamond tip,

              its single tooth. Static seeped
      out of the speakers like a tail, no,

an entire body. Its long throat a black bandage.

From a Violent Man, You Rescued Me

In an abandoned version of your childhood home, you whistle, and the dark whistles back. It is not an echo. To make sure, you say basic sentences, and basic sentences are repeated. You make your sentences increasingly more complex until you no longer hear your words repeated. Then a child-version of you emerges from the dark. The child climbs into your lap. She is clearly dying. You shout for a doctor, for this child not to die on you. But she dies, and you hear yourself screaming and you hear the dark screaming.

The Beast I Worship

The hair coiled around the drain. I bent down and pulled

    its split-end. It was long,

heavy. The drain gurgled. No, beneath the tub gurgled.

    Perhaps, from the basement—

a sound both sad and reluctant. Recently, I asked

    Is it mine? to no answer.

The hair grew thick. The pulling harder. I could hear the

    water finally draining.

It was like the coos of a baby. Unsure, I kept pulling.

    One night, I asked

my favorite question. One night, I opened my palm to

    reveal all my twisting

sinews. What did it prove? No one can detangle the logic

    of muscle, the reasoning

of what spools in the body and who started the spooling. The hair was knotted

around itself. The drain cinched it, squeezing water from the mass. Finally,

with a pop, it came free. The hair was wet-dark, covered in scum. It was like a corpse.

I turned it with my thumb and forefinger–I heard it whimper. The hair whimpered.

I could see a tiny mouth. I prodded it. The hair wrapped around my finger.

Is it mine? I asked. Was it hungry? I didn't, I couldn't know what it wanted.

The Worshipping Beast

All that whimpers isn't want.

One spring, I pulled
a reed from an oboe.
I planted it by a pond.
Instantly, it grew

dense at the water's edge.
The wind told lie after lie—

black cricket like a jewel,
black motion of a goose's

vibrating neck. I parted
the reeds but nothing
was there. I was steeped
in evening's almosts—

a symphony in a cup of water.

Snuffer's

Or whatever. I just don't want my brain there, our daughter said into her phone as she spun her keys like a handgun. In your town, they dedicated a whole section of the morgue to the brainless (and their gasping scalps). One evening at a Kroger, you made a joke to the cashier. He was 17 and believed you. We could just as easily not have had a daughter. At Snuffer's, whose meat is tender like a child's, you made the same joke to our waitress. Her sympathetic laugh, like a side of fruit, stayed with me through the meal. You told our daughter about the birds' erratic acrobatics—the tiny gaps between wingtips, between eye and beak. *What a mess when you think about it*, I mused after pointing out a moon-bleached tarp caught on barbwire. After asking if a body thrown from a vehicle would flap at the same frequency, you turned to our daughter. You said, *When I see something, I say something.*

Wounded Surgeon

As a student, I stitched
a cadaver together
while my professor
said you must

be a predator,
must see the body
as parts within
a sack of skin.

I wish I could
see the body
like that now—
how it is

right here in my hand
and also my hand.

Muzzle

I carried

a bag of groceries
up the stairs
when the baby

peeked out.
He opened
his mouth,

and I could
see teeth

working through

gums,
a tongue

running over
their tiny
crenulations.

My wife

was so happy

I didn't forget
the baby

she told me

something
very important—

about checking
receipts

so you know
what's yours.

Faithful is The Wounding

I could talk to my wife

if my wife weren't so
small and she is
very small.

My wife runs
around the bedframe
like a marathon

but she never
comes to bed.

If she isn't tired
then I'm not tired.

I want to talk to my wife

about all my desires
for her to be no longer
small but her little
radio is too loud

as she does aerobics
on the nightstand
I watch my wife

How can I
compete with her

our daughter our son
wrapped in the exercise
bands of her arms

The Old City

We carried our bodies through the old city

to the abandoned mall. Its shattered windows
sunk their shrapnel teeth into the moon.

I was crying. Yes, I was crying.
I tried to say I wouldn't hurt a fly.
Behind us, cars exploded

into thousands of tinier cars.
They dragged the bodies within them
through the night like a hive tossed
between two boys, friends

testing each other's courage—the impending sting.

The mall glowed in the red wake
of traffic. The world was warm,
so I wanted to take

off my clothes, let them fall
on the earth's muscled back.

I couldn't say *hurt myself*, and I didn't
for a long time. For a very long time

the sky shook out its fur above us.
It ribboned from the streetlights

dotting the parking lot. Our bodies,

once asleep, were now bees
bursting from the mouth

of the hive that housed them.

Sometimes My Phone Doesn't Ring

Once everyone I lied to congregated on the left side of a room
        I lived in

for five months. I was
older but in many ways new
to the pain that could be
stolen from other people.

Once a woman killed herself in the bedroom we shared.

Some of us push our words
painfully into place
with a single horsehair brush.
Others, well, there are others too.

Sometimes I want simple things—a plot in a graveyard to visit
        and visit, a child

cutting her own hair, a line
of holes telling me where a stud sits.

Sometimes I replay her voicemail: *come get your junk and pull*
        out all the nails

you pounded into our walls,
you piece of shit.

Faithful is The Wounding

I was raised on roots softened with heat
and butter, on glossolalia—the tongue's

sable crown—on knowing the Lord's strict
unknowableness. I saw what I could not

know lift my bed sheets. In the cellar,
I watched flies swell the roots' flesh
until their wings burst out. They dropped

me into my bed, into the smell of a man
who knew me. Yes, I believe I believed.
What else was there to do

when my mouth's uses mystified my mouth?

Without Recourse

You stroke your hair and pass over a lump in the center of your head. You brush your hair to reveal your nose, your opened mouth. You inhale. You've made a tragic mistake. From the corners of your room, the flies rush in. You swallow their wings, their empty bottle bodies. Your eyes do not blink as you float around the room.

Chanted Everywhere Other Than The Gravesite

I sang the name with my leaking
mouth. *Yitgadal, v'itkadesh...*

From the faucet, forgetfulness. The ambulance

in the chest galloped through
the body's maelstrom. I was there,
and I was not

the skull's blank page. In the sink, the many liquid moons

gathered to splash the morning's face
as if this were a dream before a shave.

Someone Else's Baby

At the party, you held their baby. They were in another room with their friends. When you looked at their baby, you heard the howling within. You wish you could explain how it felt—that little heart beating in your hand long after they swept the baby away.

Like a Ribbon, Unspooling Forever

She hides behind the door
her hands make

across her face
When she peeks
out I giggle.

She hides again
I become a tree

that shakes
as something
rushes by it.

Her eyes roll
across the horizon.
Her breathing is heavy.

I am far away.
I am a house.

A person walks out

of my opening
door.

Still Alive

In a field, a black foal
catches the moon along
its sway-back. Its legs
are knobbed. Its inky mane
sloshes over the inkwell
of its awkward body.
It turns. It wears my face—
my green eyes, my smile
under the lopsided moon
hanging from two
invisible hooks.

Invasive

You stare at the river from the bridge. Your chin rests on the metal railing. Wires suspend you. They shoot into the sky. You feel the bridge shake. When the wobbling becomes more pronounced, you hear the footsteps— marching toward you, fresh from the blackberry patch, an army of children, their mouths smeared into a constant opening.

Faithful is The Wounding

My husband sleeps. In the garage,
I smash the cans in the recycling.

I float into our room.
He is a lump

under the covers. I remember
when he destroyed

the porch furniture with his maul.
Each crack opened my eyes.

I pick him up, and he unravels
into a sheet. I look out

the window. My husband scurries
under the porch. He slips

down the storm drain. *Good
riddance*, I think and tuck myself in.

All Pigeons Were Once Called Doves

It happens sometimes.
One bird breaks
against the bay window,

and the mind smears
the thump into a grey bruise.

Then the children,
who hunger for cruelty,
rush to the window to see

it. One says he sees
a pigeon with a broken neck.

The adults shield them
from what they can,
but one day a bird breaks

against the bay window.
It spreads feathers

over the ground, ruining
whatever tranquility

could be pried from the view.

Then the day bruises
with parents telling the children

that sometimes this happens,
that it was just a bird
and no need to cry for a bird.

One of the children says
it was a dove,

but he doesn't know
for certain. He is new
and rushes into things

like a young soldier
carrying his shield behind him.

To Be Cut Into Halves

To you, the day is ruined. Under the bay window, the bird bruises the ground with its body's lump and feathers. When you think back, the bay window isn't certain. Neither the thump. But the bird, yes, the bird. It broke against these things. It spreads its feathers under the shrubs. The bay window shielded you from the bird's broken neck. But you can imagine. You can pry the ground up with your fingernails, smear the earth across your face. You say you found a pigeon. But this isn't certain. Your mind clouds. You are the parent to each feathered thought.

Snow Baby

I look
at the snow

baby. It sits

in the gap
between
streetlights,

a grey smudge
on the night's

turtleneck.
An irritant

in the open

eye. It
followed
me home.

When I run
my bath

I picture

the snow baby

sliding down
the street
with the sun.

Muzzle

A black Accord
with its blinker on.

I sigh;
my daughter says

everything behind
inching toward

an empty space.
We do not move.

She waves the car
into our lane

raises the volume's
invisible fist.

Faithful is The Wounding

Bending off a side street, we sucked
down our cinnamoned whiskey—

its luster grew in the mason jars
of our stomachs. The summer we tried
to free ourselves with red wax

sealed bottles, I played dead
in the corners of the swimming pool.

We filled it with concrete after
I fished a pregnant opossum
from the filter. Its fur peeled

off, and naked it looked
so much like the child

growing inside.

Some Light Can Never Be Seen

In the basement, ultraviolet coiled around
the dancing teens, their green teeth

held in the noose of their parted lips.
I poured a bag of Cheetos into a bowl

as my daughter stared at bulbs emitting
the unseeable. The snacks glowed

like a television recently turned off.
Upstairs, a woman held a tangled string

of sighing lights and believed the pattern
of light and dark to be a response

to her questions: *Are you there? You are,
aren't you?* The show was smeared

with Vaseline and synthesizers. It ended
with something inside pulsing out.

I waved to my daughter. She tried
on the face of a stranger. If only

I had an X-ray, the short-cut into
ourselves, I would recognize what is

metastasizing within her. I would know
what to look for. Earlier, I asked

a question; my daughter said, *Mind
your own business.* My jaws fused.

Strange about messages made in pieces:
a broken glass and a song on the radio,

a shirt worn at a thrift store and a note
penned in a book—not what it says, no,

the way the letters coil around themselves.

Thanks

I would like to thank the following people, without whom this manuscript would certainly not exist: Marcus Myers, Sebastian Paramo, Andrew Reeves, Ruth Williams, Ashley Roach-Freman, Sugar le Fae, Hadara Bar-Nadav, Jose Araguz, Paige Lockhart and Leanna Bales.

I would also like to thank the following people who helped me stay with poetry even when things seemed bleakest: Susan Aizenberg, Jonny Boothe, Deanna McElhattan, Mathias Svalina, Jordan Stemplemen, Rebecca Hazelton, Crista Siglin, Zach Voss, Steph French, Teresa Leggard, Seren Bradley, Rowen Foster, Andrew Johnson, Whitney Terrell, Lauren Stookey, Jon Miller, Barbara Varanka, Blaze Christopher, Michael Sikkema, Nick Gulig, Mina Macheret, Wayne Miller, Kathryn Nuernberger, Megan Arlett, Jim Redmond, Bruce Bond, Austin Price, Adamska Rakhilkina, and all the editors who believed in these poems along the way.

Thank you to Jen Harris and Simone Muench who saw something in these poems. Also, special thanks to Richard Siken, my editor at JackLeg, for not knowing and showing me how to not know with him.

And thank you, most of all, to my parents, who always encouraged me to embrace life's incongruencies.

Acknowledgments

Barrow Street: "Like a Ribbon, Unspooling Forever"

Bennington Review: "Someone Else's Baby" "Errands"

Birmingham Poetry Review: "The Histories"

BOAAT: "Boxcutter"

Boston Review: "Wounded Surgeon"

Broadsided: "The Nature of Punishment," "Nightride" (also published in the *Jeans! An Homage to Denim Anthology*)

Cincinnati Review: "Folding Coats"

Colorado Review: "A Cicada Sings At Night to Avoid Predators" (a winner of the 2018 AWP Intro Awards)

concis: "Invasive"

CutBank: "Stillborn"

A Dozen Nothing: "Apologies Are Unnecessary," "Chanted Everywhere Other Than The Gravesite"

elsewhere: "Helicopter"

GASHER Journal: "Within Him," "In Traffic"

Gigantic Sequins: "If You Say It's a Dream, Then It Doesn't Count"

The Grist: "And They Shrank From Coming Near Him"

Guernica: "Wither" (included in *The New Anthology of Contemporary Surrealist and Magical Realist Poetry*)

Hobart: "The Worshipping Beast"

HOOT: "Still Alive"

Image: "Such are The Rituals"

The Journal: "After Multiple Citations, I Rake The Lawn"

Juked: "The Bedroom," "Muzzle"

Mid-American Review: "From a Violent Man, You Rescued Me"

Ninth Letter Online: "Without Recourse"

North Dakota Quarterly: "Some Light Can Never Be Seen"

PANK!: "Hanger"

The Pinch: "By The Rivers of Omaha"

Pleiades: "The Small Wife," "Sometimes My Phone Doesn't Ring" (winner of the 2017 Stanley Hanks Memorial Poetry Prize)

Portland Review: "Devil in the Backyard"

Prairie Schooner: "Snow Baby"

Quarterly West: "The Old City"

RHINO: "All Pigeons Were Once Called Doves," "To Be Cut in Halves"

Salamander: "The Beast I Worship" [Nominated for *The Best New Poets Anthology*]

Salt Hill Journal: "Faithful is The Wounding"

South Carolina Review: "It Doesn't Sound Good at All"

Tinderbox Poetry: "Own"

Typo: "I Want to Be Kicked in The Head"

Vassar Review: "Looking for Someone Who's Not Around"

Whiskey Island: "Take All The Time You Need," "Tar"

JACKLEG PRESS

V. Joshua Adams, Mark Baumgartner, Scott Shibuya Brown, Michael Chin, Chloe Clark, Rivka Clifton, Brittney Corrigan, Jessica Cuello, Barbara Cully, Allison Cundiff, Curious Theatre Branch, Neil de la Flor, Genevieve DeGuzman, Suzanne Frischkorn, Victoria Garza, Reginald Gibbons, Joachim Glage, Caroline Goodwin, Brett Hanley, Kathryn Kruse, Brigitte Lewis, Jenny Magnus, DK McCutchen, Jean McGarry, Rita Mookerjee, Mamie Morgan, Alexis Orgera, Zach Powers, Karen Rigby, Jo Salas, Maureen Seaton, Kristine Snodgrass, Cornelia Spelman, Peter Stenson, Melissa Studdard, Gemini Wahhaj, Megan Weiler, David Welch, Cassandra Whitaker, David Wesley Williams

jacklegpress.org

www.ingramcontent.com/pod-product-compliance
Lightning Source LLC
Chambersburg PA
CBHW031246120626
46545CB00007B/2679